The Parent's
SURVIVAL
Handbook

First published in Great Britain in 2002

10 9 8 7 6 5 4 3 2 1

First published by
Ebury Press
Random House
20 Vauxhall Bridge Road
London SW1 2SA

Random House Australia (Pty) Limited
20 Alfred Street, Milsons Point
Sydney
New South Wales 2061, Australia

Random House New Zealand Limited
18 Poland Road, Glenfield, Auckland 10
New Zealand

Random House South Africa (Pty) Limited
Endulini, 5A Jubilee Road
Parktown 2193
South Africa

Random House UK Limited Reg. No. 954009

www.randomhouse.co.uk

A CIP catalogue record for this book is available from the
British Library

ISBN 0091885280

Papers used by Ebury Press are natural, recyclable products
made from wood grown in sustainable forests

Printed and bound in Denmark by Nørhaven Paperback A/S

The Parent's
SURVIVAL
Handbook

ROHAN CANDAPPA

EBURY PRESS

*For the Big Fella, who is a dream
come true.*

*And for Charmain, who helped our
dreams come true.*

INTRODUCTION

No-one tells you what it's really like. So you stumble into parenthood with the hopelessly idealistic expectation that it'll be filled with 'oohs' and 'aahs'. Unfortunately it's more likely to be filled with 'oh-no's' and 'arghhs'. And several other choice expressions often spelled with the odd asterisk or two in the middle.

Look at it another way and parenting is the kind of job that should be seriously examined by the Health and Safety at Work people, an Industrial Tribunal, and The United Nations Commission on Human Rights. I mean, in what other job would you have a boss who could get you to work at any hour of the day or night, who you had to wait on hand and foot (and bottom), and whose clothing, food and physical need you had to provide?

This guide is but my feeble attempt to try and tip the scales a little bit back in your favour. Frankly, it won't be of much use. Because nothing is. You see, the real truth about parenting is that you just have to get in there and muddle through as best you can. And hope that the kids don't sue you when they're old enough to hire a lawyer.

Good Luck.

What the Other Books Won't Tell You ...

YOU'LL NOTICE THE CRYING FIRST

Experts suggest that your baby is likely to cry every night for 12 weeks after birth. Especially if suffering from colic. Bizarrely, when they eventually become teenagers you'll look back on this as a relatively peaceful, happy time.

IN A TECHNOLOGICAL WORLD
WHERE ALL THINGS SEEM
POSSIBLE, THERE IS AN
ABSOLUTE LIMIT TO MAN'S
INGENUITY BEYOND WHICH WE
WILL NEVER REACH

All nappies leak.

WHO'S GOING TO STAY UP TO WATCH THE END OF THAT?

Your views of movies on television will subtly alter. In the past you berated TV programmers when they scheduled films to start at 11pm. Now you'll do the same when they start at 9pm.

AN EXERCISE TO HELP YOU LEARN HOW TO COPE

Fill a pillow case with several bags of sugar. Strap it to your leg below knee level. Then practise doing all your usual, day-to-day, kitchen-based activities. It's good preparation for when your child hits that charming 'clingy' stage.

25-7

Some careers, situations or lifestyles are so relentless that the term '24-7' was coined to describe the fact that they went on 24 hours a day, seven days a week.

Parenting a baby or a small child, especially if the little darling is your first, is an altogether more gruelling affair. Hence the term '25-8'. As in parenting is something you find yourself doing 25 hours a day, eight days a week.

VIDEO RECORDERS.
THE SHOCKING TRUTH

You know how you used to curse the manufacturer of your VCR every time you had to scrabble around on your hands and knees to set the damned thing? It is only when you have a baby or small child around that you realise the true extent of their evil ways.

That's because videos are designed to be located at floor level, with a very appealing letterbox opening that no small person can resist. Inevitably, your VCR will get broken. And you will have to buy another one.

It's a ploy joyously referred to around the massive swimming pools of the MDs of VCR manufacturing companies as 'built-in childolescence'.

PARENTHOOD. YOU'LL LEARN A LOT, YOU'LL PICK UP A LOT

As the parent of a small child, the main thing you'll learn is that you spend most of your time picking things up off the floor.

WHITE CLOTHES FOR SMALL CHILDREN
Whose bright idea was that?

THE SHARPEST CUTTING IMPLEMENT KNOWN TO MAN
A baby's fingernails.

THE INVERSE PROPORTION RULE OF TOYS

Toys will be played with in precise inverse proportion to their monetary cost.

NATURE OR NURTURE. ARE THOSE REALLY THE ONLY TWO OPTIONS?

For many years now the 'nature-nurture' debate has exercised the finest minds in the world of child development. In a nutshell, the debate comes down to whether it is a child's genetic make-up or the nurturing they receive from their parents that is the key determinant of their personality, behaviour, ability to refold a Sunday broadsheet newspaper later on in life, etc.

However, there is a glaring flaw in the parameters of this debate that

18

any parent will recognise. It is this: at regular intervals your child will display behaviour that is neither natural, nor learned.

For example, I have watched almost every wildlife programme there's ever been on TV and I have yet to witness any creature taking tissues from a box and ripping them up for no apparent reason. So it's not nature. And my partner and I have never done it. So it's not nurture.

So, if it's not nature and it's not nurture, then what is it?

Have you seen *The Exorcist*?

IS THE GLASS HALF EMPTY OR HALF FULL?

There are those who see the glass as half empty. And there are those who see the glass as half full. The former are categorised as pessimists. The latter as optimists.

To the experienced parent of a small child this simplistic analysis misses the most relevant part of the scenario. For them, the glass is both half empty and half full.

The half-empty part of the glass inevitably leads the mind to ponder where the Ribena that was in there has got to. Is it:

A. In the child?
B. On the pale beige carpet they've just had cleaned?

The half-full part of the glass leads the mind to wonder whether it's worth leaving the rest of the Ribena with the child given that they've either:

1. Drunk half of it and so are bound to lose interest in drinking the second half, which makes it more likely that the un-drunk half will be carelessly knocked over.

2. Already spilt half of it on to the pale beige carpet. So why not quit while you're behind and retrieve what's left before that falls too.

All of which leads me to my division of the world of parents into:

A. Pessimists.

B. Serious Pessimists

SLEEPING PATTERNS

Yeah, right.

BATH TIME
Your aim is to get them as clean as possible. Their aim is to get you as wet as possible. If most days the result is a draw, then you're doing well.

FEEDING. THE BASICS
Food should go in one end, and come out the other. Any alternative arrangement is to be discouraged.

ON THE SHOULDERS OF MENTAL PYGMIES

Never forget when carrying a small child on your shoulders that the combined height of both of you is greater than the height of just you on your own. It is particularly apposite to remember this when going through doorways.

ON CRYING AGAIN

A certain amount is to be expected. But try not to let it get out of hand, especially in public, as it will only confuse and embarrass your child.

AN AGE-OLD DEBATE RESOLVED

Over the centuries, poets, academics and philosophers have pondered on the sweetest words ever uttered by man. Could it be the poetry of the King James bible, the elegant simplicity of Einstein's $E=mc^2$, Shakespeare's immortal 'Shall I compare thee to a summer's day?' Well, it's none of these. The sweetest words known to man (and more usually to woman) are those blissful words you hear yourself groaning to your partner at three in the morning when yet another wail rents the air. 'It's your turn'.

THE SLIDE RULE

The Slide Rule states that in any given playground or indoor, excessively padded, playground-like facility, it is far more interesting for a small child to climb up the slide (and I'm not talking about the steps here) than it is for them to slide down it.

Incidentally, shouting 'Don't Climb Up The Slide!' at the top of your voice at your budding Bonnington will do little more than redouble their efforts to conquer this particular peak, in this particular fashion.

It must be noted that as well as The Slide Rule there is also The Slide

Rule Sudden Impact Addendum.
This states that the higher the slide,
the more imperative it is for your
small child to climb up the slide part
at the precise moment when a much
larger child is hurtling down it.

THE HIDDEN PITFALLS
IN CHILDREN'S SONGS

Charming though they are, children's songs can be a hidden minefield for the unsuspecting parent. The problem is that the words of any particular song can be subtly different in different places. Sing the wrong words on the wrong occasion and you will end up feeling as out of place as a bacon buttie at a Bar Mitzvah.

ANOTHER OF THOSE ANNOYING LAWS

The propensity of a small child or baby to eat any particular food is in direct inverse proportion to how long it took to prepare that food.

DUMMIES

Damned if you do, damned if you don't.

THE DIMINISHING RETURNS YOU'LL ENCOUNTER ON THE PHOTOGRAPHIC FRONT

This is the way it works

When your first-born is first born everything they do and everything about them will be greeted with 'oohs' and 'aahs' and the incessant sound of a camera shutter going off. Your logic will be that your loved one's every development is significant, hence worthy of being preserved. And if the moments aren't significant per se, they are just so damn cute that who can resist taking a picture?

The end result is A. a rapidly growing mountain of photographs with which to bore visitors and B. that shares in Boots (or wherever else you get your pictures developed) will soar.

Then your second-born is born. And try as you might to be equally as interested in their developments and general all-round cuteness, the photographic evidence to the contrary will be piling up all around you. Or more accurately, it won't be piling up because you won't take nearly as many pictures.

And what happens if there's a third-born? Well, they'll be lucky to get a trip to a photo booth to get a passport photo done.

'WHY DOES THAT ALWAYS HAPPEN?'

When doing up the poppers on a sleep suit at bedtime, it is an absolute rule that there will always be one popper left over at the end.

IT'S TIME SOMEONE TOLD THE ASTROPHYSICISTS

There is a stronger gravitational pull in the universe than that exerted by a black hole. It's the irresistible attractive force that overcomes a new parent when anywhere in the vicinity of Baby Gap.

AND YOU THOUGHT BILL GATES' NEW PAD COST A LOT TO CONSTRUCT

Lego is the most expensive building material known to man. In comparison, the finest Carrara marble is as cheap as chipboard.

WHY YOU'LL ALWAYS BE LATE WHEREVER YOU'RE GOING

When travelling anywhere with small children, always remember it's not the actual journey that takes the most time, it's the getting out of the house.

CARS

Whatever car you own before the birth of your first child, sell it and buy a bigger one. Preferably, get a people carrier. Ideally, get an HGV. That's because wherever you go after the birth of your first baby you'll inevitably carry enough stuff to restock a small branch of Mothercare.

IN A SPIN
You will be amazed how much washing even the smallest of small people can generate.

CHILD LOCKS ON CUPBOARDS
On the whole a good idea, but in the end even an averagely intelligent child will figure how to get out of the cupboard.

QUIBBLING SIBLINGS. (OR HOW MINOR DISPUTES CAN RAPIDLY ESCALATE INTO ALL, OUT WAR)

Like many a major international conflict, trouble can often start over a seemingly innocuous incident. For example:

1. Sibling A has a juice bottle.
2. Sibling A has drunk their fill of said juice and puts the bottle down.
3. Sibling B reaches for the discarded bottle to help themselves to a drink.
4. All hell breaks loose.

In the world of the parent this conflict makes no sense whatsoever. After all, sibling A has finished with the juice, so why shouldn't sibling B drink some? That's because, as in so many conflicts, what's actually at stake here is not what seems to be at stake, but something much more important.

Just as the Gulf War wasn't a war about democracy in the Gulf, but about oil supplies to the West, this dispute isn't about who's drinking the juice, but about who controls the supply of juice. Hence the dispute is, fundamentally, about power.

The only useful advice I can supply in such circumstances is that you read Machiavelli's *The Prince*, Sun Tzu's *The Art Of War*, and watch that bit in *Lawrence Of Arabia* where Lawrence and his Bedouin warriors sweep down onto the stricken train shouting 'Take No Prisoners!'
Then you might have an outside chance of handling the situation.

TANTRUMS

They are ugly, irritating and, in public places, can be extremely embarrassing, but sometimes they're the only way to get your child to do what you want them to.

LIFT-THE-FLAP BOOKS

A complete misnomer. Tear-the-flap books is a far more accurate description.

IN CHARGE, BUT NOT IN CONTROL
Better get used to the feeling.

INTERIOR DESIGN
There is only one style of home decor that can accommodate large amounts of brightly coloured plastic without compromising its aesthetic appeal. Pop Art. So unless you've had Peter Blake or Jeff Koons in doing your lounge, just accept the fact that any attempt to tastefully secrete your child's stuff around your abode is doomed to failure.

SHOES
These are small and easily lost. Also most young children can grow out of a pair of shoes in the time it takes you to get them back from the shoe shop. Hence, if you sat down and worked out their price on a cost-per-wear basis, they would undoubtedly represent less value than that pair of Jimmy Choo's you so coveted in last month's Vogue.

A GAGGLE OF GEESE
The correct collective noun for a group of three or more small children is a shriek.

PSY. OPS

Psy. Ops. is short for Psychological Operations. This is a division of baby/small-child behaviour that they employ in order to break your will as a parent. If this sounds an altogether too bleak an assessment of your beloveds motivations and abilities maybe the following brief list of fairly basic Psy. Ops. will give you pause for thought:

TACTIC ONE:
SLEEP DEPRIVATION

A classic ploy. 'Security' forces the world over have long known that depriving an individual of sleep is one of the surest ways of weakening that individual's resolve. Keep up the tactic day after day and week after week, and the victim is soon reduced to a barely functioning zombie, willing to do anything if you just let them sleep. Sound familiar?

TACTIC TWO:
THE OLD 'GOOD BABY/BAD BABY' ROUTINE

This is similar to the 'Good Cop/Bad Cop' routine that police employ to get suspects to admit to a crime. The key difference here is that both contrasting personas are not manifest in two individuals, but in the one baby. Your one baby. The end result is the same.

A combination of alternating trust and fear that will leave you disorientated and vulnerable.

45

TACTIC THREE:
WHEN MUSIC ISN'T THE FOOD OF LOVE

In the not too recent past, the military forces of the United States were charged with the task of getting General Noriega out of the presidential palace where he had holed up, without resorting to an armed assault. They plumped for an altogether more frightening approach. They set up vast speakers around the presidential compound and played annoying songs, at full volume, over and over and over again. The poor man didn't stand a chance. He soon staggered out with his arms in the air. It's a response you may well sympathise with when trapped on a long car journey with a small child who wails like a banshee. Especially when you make even the slightest attempt to remove the cassette from the tape player that's serenading you with the delights of 'The Wheels On The Bus', 'The Grand Old Duke Of York' and 'Hickory, Dickory, Bloody Dock'.

A WORD OF WARNING ABOUT BOUNCY CASTLES

The smaller the child, the higher they bounce.

STEP ON IT

When creeping carefully out of your baby's dark room after finally getting said baby off to sleep, just accept the fact that your foot will land on the room's one creaky floorboard.

THE LOOK OF LOVE
Every now and again you will catch sight of your child looking at you with an almost transcendentally blissful look of joy on their face. For the briefest of moments you will bask happily in their total love for you. Then the wind will change direction and you'll nose out what's really been going on.

A MONEY SAVING TIP

If you invest in a sandpit for your garden, please don't make the mistake of buying sand for it at the same time. Instead, just empty your child's shoes and turn ups into it each time they return from a trip to the sandpit at the playground. After three or four such trips you will have easily accumulated enough free sand to reconstruct a one to one scale model of Bondai Beach.

'BUT IT HASN'T RAINED FOR SEVEN MONTHS!'

When letting a small child loose in a park on a sunny day, always remember that every single one of them has the innate ability to find a puddle in the Sahara. So they will inevitably return to you in a somewhat muddy state.

CHOCOLATE

Before feeding any small child any form of chocolate, melt some of it in your hand and smear it over your own clothes. It saves time.

THE ENDLESS BUFFET

To a crawling baby or an inquisitive small child, the floor in your home is nothing more than a vast smorgasbord of possibilities waiting to be experienced. Hence anything lying around is fair game for collection and attempted consumption. The same, rather more worryingly, is also true of the outside world.

THE REAL REASON PEOPLE HAVE MORE THAN ONE CHILD

Well, you've got all the stuff. You might as well get a decent amount of use out of it.

THE MOUTH

The mouth is not a specific location but, rather like 'the north' in weather reports, is a vague region. Hence foodstuffs that, theoretically, should exclusively enter the mouth are all too often to be found scattered over a wide facial, and indeed bodily, area.

BOREDOM

Small children are easily bored. You try to interest them in some activity or game and they'll be engaged for a few minutes, then lose all interest. Well, I don't really know how to break this to you, but actually it's not the activity that they're bored with.

ONE OF THE GREATEST PLEASURES OF BEING A PARENT REVEALED

It's that moment of elation you experience after you hear a child throwing a mega tantrum, and you realise that it isn't yours.

AND YOU THOUGHT THAT SEX WAS THE MOST SATISFYING ACTIVITY THAT YOU COULD GET UP TO IN BED

It's not. It's sleep. You will soon reach the state where you would happily swap the most earth – shattering, multi-orgasmic experience of your life for eight hours of uninterrupted blissful oblivion.

58

WHAT DELIA, JAMIE AND NIGELLA MISSED OUT

Fine though these purveyors of the culinary arts may be, there is one arena of cooking skills that none of them has, as yet, covered. I speak of what the French, I believe, refer to as *La Culinaire de Seul Main*. Or as we say round my neck *des bois*, One-Handed Cooking.

Before you are encumbered with a baby this will seem a bizarre and somewhat pointless area to master. But post-encumberment you'll wish you'd practised the art.

It all becomes relevant in the kitchen because babies invariably save their most irritating wails for the moments you'd set aside for actually cooking something. No toy will placate them, no distraction distract them. Your only sanity preserving option is to hoist and carry while you cook.

So what, precisely, can you cook one-handed? I'm afraid my achievements stretch no further than toast, cup-a-soup and chocolate Hob Nobs. So in strict nutritional terms it wasn't what you'd call a balanced diet. (Incidentally, in case anyone should be tempted I really wouldn't recommend dunking a chocolate

Hob Nob into a chicken and leek cup-a soup. Fusion cooking is a concept best left to the experts).

All of which leads me to conclude that if there's anyone out there who wants to try their hand (just the one) at coming up with a cook book of *La Culinaire de Seul Main* they will make an absolute killing.

A POINT OF EMPATHY

Small children get easily frustrated by things they can't, or aren't allowed to do on account of them being small children.

Ironically, you too will get easily frustrated by things you can't do on account of having small children.

THE BEST WAY TO GO ON HOLIDAY WITH THEM

Pack a small bag with all their favourite toys. Drop the bag off, with the child, at your mother's place en route to the airport. Collect bag and child after you return, tanned and rested, from your holiday. (Well, isn't she always saying she'd love to see them more often.)

RETURNING TO WORK

Oh right, so looking after the kids all day while you swan off to the office and have lunch with your mates and your secretary and just 'a quick drink with the lads after work', stagger home and bang around the kitchen trying to make yourself something to eat, then come to bed and snore so loudly that I'm up half the night, isn't work?

(Sorry about that, bit of a raw nerve. I really must get a decent night's sleep tonight. Let's just move on to the next page).

64

WHY FIGHT IT?

You know that cupboard under the sink where you keep the bleach, the extra washing up liquid and all that manky cleaning stuff that you used once but didn't really work and for some obscure reason you refuse to throw away? Well, use that cupboard to store toys. After all, it's the cupboard that small children will be the most insistent on opening.

HOW MUCH TELEVISION SHOULD SMALL CHILDREN WATCH?

Experts suggest that one hour's television viewing per day is more than enough for a young child. Don't you just hate experts?

ONE OF THE SECRETS OF BEING A GOOD PARENT

Whenever another parent asks you how much television you allow your child to watch, always halve the actual figure.

ON THE BENDINESS OF BABIES

Babies are very flexible. However, despite the recent craze for babigami, or the ancient Japanese art of baby folding, among mothers on the west coast of the States, it is a practice whose benefits most medical doctors doubt.

JUST ONE OF THE REASONS WHY THE BIBLE ISN'T A GREAT CHILD-REARING MANUAL

It may well be easier for a camel to get through the eye of a needle than for a rich man to get into the kingdom of heaven, but none of that cuts any ice with a baby determined to squeeze their way around the back of a sofa.

POCKET MUMMY

Remember how when you were a kid, after weeks and weeks of playing during the endless summer holidays, your mother would suggest that maybe it was about time you emptied your pockets of all the accumulated booty you had saved because it was interesting, or because you'd finish eating it later, or because you wanted to share it with your best friend, or because you didn't want to share it with your best friend or a hundred other reasons?

So you'd tip out the contents of said pockets and you'd find sweets, and biscuits, and half-sucked sweets, and half-chewed biscuits, and small toys, and small bits broken off big toys, and snotty handkerchiefs, and snotty tissues, and half-sucked sweets stuck in snotty tissues, and all manner of seemingly indiscriminate, useless and arbitrary detritus.

And you know how it's often been said that parenthood brings back the child in you? Well, this is one of the ways it brings it back. And it brings it back, specifically, to your pockets.

THE ONE THAT GOT AWAY

At some point in your career as the parent of a small child you will encounter what can only be sensibly referred to as The Renegade Poo. This is usually a small, perfectly shaped and subtly hued turd whose only flaw is that it is not anywhere that it should be. It is not in the nappy, it is not in the potty, it is not in the toilet. It is somewhere else. It might be found behind the sofa. Or in the bedclothes. Or even in the toe of a Wellington boot. And try as you might, you will not be able to fathom out how it got there or when it got there. Who got it there, however, will never be in doubt.

Believe me, when confronted with such a situation it is best not to contemplate the possibilities for too long. That way madness lies. Instead, just dispose of said unwanted item and chalk it up to experience. And should you happen to catch the eye of the perpetrator, look carefully and behind the blameless innocence that will no doubt greet you. There will be just a trace of triumph.

EVOLUTION

Scientific research will soon show that human beings are not only descended from apes, but also from lemmings. This explains the urge all babies have to head for the edge of high places, beds, tables, sofas for example and totter precariously.

BE PREPARED AT MEALTIMES

Think ahead. Only feed your baby food that matches the colour of the clothes that you are wearing.

BITING THE HAND THAT FEEDS YOU

And you thought that was just an expression, didn't you?

A WORD OF WARNING

When anyone asks you how your baby is they actually only want an answer that lasts up to one minute. If you must show pictures, limit yourself to two. Break the 'one minute/two picture rule' and you run the risk of losing all your friends.

WHERE'S THE CHANGING BAG?

Buy one changing bag for each room of your house, and one more for the car. Extravagant, I know, but trust me on this one.

POST-NATAL DEPRESSION

This describes the state of mind you get into when, having given birth to your child and been stuck at home with them for quite some considerable time, you realise that the highlight of your day is the arrival of the post.

WAVING BYE-BYE

It's one of the first interactions that you and your baby will achieve. And it is very charming. But while you're going all gooey inside with pride as your little darling waves their chubby little hand at you there's one thing you should consider. They really mean it.

'LET'S TALK ABOUT...'

Oh the joys of communication. At last to be able to know what's going on inside their pretty little heads. Not that much of it will make any sense. And there'll be occasions when your child will fix you with a stare of an intensity that could only be matched by Jeremy Paxman cornering a nervous junior minister, and expect you to join in a conversation that is as clear as a bowl of bouillabaisse.

There will be verbs involved. And nouns. And even the occasional adjective. (But don't get excited about the adjective thing as it's most likely to be the word 'big' and very unlikely to be, for example, 'pinteresque'). And none of it will be in the least comprehensible. But it is crucial for your child's development of language skills that you act as if you understand every single syllable.

To help you to this end I list a selection of useful words and phrases that you can deploy in these oh-so-important one-to-one chats:

'Oh...'

'Oh?'

'Oh!'

'You don't say?'

'That's very interesting'

'Go and tell mummy/daddy

(delete as applicable) about it'.
'No, I think that you'll find that the
film was actually called *Battleship
Potemkin* not *Butterball Pumpkin*.'

TV RESCHEDULING
You'll video a lot more TV programs.
(Not that you'll ever watch them).

'AGAIN, AGAIN!'

Words you'll learn to hate. Whether they're uttered at the end reading an inane book, watching a mind-numbing video or after the umpteenth time of some back-breaking lifting and swinging game you stupidly thought would be fun. These words are the stuff of nightmares for any parent. I blame the Teletubbies.

WHAT NOT TO SAY IF YOU'VE
BEEN OUT ALL DAY FOR
WHATEVER REASON AND
RETURN TO YOUR PARTNER WHO
IS SHATTERED FROM LOOKING
AFTER YOUR CHILDREN ALL DAY,
ESPECIALLY WHEN IT'S BEEN
RAINING AND THEY HAVEN'T
BEEN ABLE TO GO OUTSIDE.
'God, I've had an awful day.'

THE TRAIN AND TUNNEL METHOD OF CHILD FEEDING: A FEW THOUGHTS

If you think this analogy through, a few problems soon become apparent. After all, if the spoon is the train, and the mouth is the tunnel, that means the foodstuffs are the passengers and they've been left in the tunnel while the train reverses out, picks up more passengers, then returns to deposit them too. I mean, what kind of way is that to run a railway?

AN ALGEBRAIC EXPLANATION OF THE ESCAPE VELOCITY OF A SMALL CHILD

You and your child are in room X, defined by a set of parameters Y, where there is only one exit Z. Unfortunately, by the time you've got this far with the equation your child will be out of exit Z, have rushed through rooms A, B, C and D and knocked over and smashed the most expensive breakable item in room E. That's how fast the blighters move.

CHILDPROOFING YOUR HOME

No matter how hard you try, and how diligently you seek out every potential hazard, there will be one incredibly obscure danger that you fail to discover. Strangely, this particular danger will be the one your child will home in on unerringly the split second that your back is turned.

CHILDPROOFING YOUR HOME. AN ALTERNATIVE ATTACK

You need:

A. A large sheet of two inch thick foam rubber.

B. 3 rolls of insulation tape.

Method: Wrap item A around your child. Secure with items B. Only remove when child leaves home to get married.

PARENTHOOD AND
THE SUPERNATURAL

One of the most surprising aspects of
the whole parenthood malarkey is
the way that it gets you to re-
evaluate your relationship with the
supernatural. Now I don't care if you
have a PhD in scepticism and are of
the firmest conviction that there is a
solid scientific explanation for every
phenomenon that occurs in the
universe. Because all of this cuts no
ice when it comes to one of the great
mysteries of life that you, as a
parent, will inevitably experience.

This is the fact that every now and

again Toys Just Disappear. You can turn your home upside down, inside out and even back to front, but the elusive toy will remain resolutely absent. Whether it is, for example, Cat, Red Bear or Woody that is Missing In Action, no logical re-tracing of events will furnish any clue as to where they have gone.

All of which means that you are only left with the illogical explanation:

The Toy Poltergeist.

HOME DECOR HINT

If you plan to re-carpet your abode
before the arrival of a small person,
invest in a design whose pattern
resembles various crushed foodstuffs
livened up with stains and dribbles
of a variety of shapes, sizes and
colours.

RELUCTANT EATERS

If your child is a reluctant eater try relocating your meal to a typical busy British restaurant at lunchtime, where the cheery enthusiasm and admirable patience of the staff, management and customers will undoubtedly make the whole experience one to savour.

ALL FINGERS AND FUMBS

Okay, so when you were young you could do a Rubik's cube in less than thirty seconds, blindfolded whilst singing the harmonies from 'Bohemian Rhapsody'. And maybe you can do that *Twin Peaks* tying a knot in the stalk of a cherry with your tongue thing. And maybe you can even get the shrink wrap off a new blank video without resorting to a knife from the the kitchen drawer and a surfeit of bad language. But all of these undoubtedly admirable feats of dexterity pale before the Ultimate Challenge of Nimbleness.

I speak, of course, of getting all a small (and often wriggling) child's fingers into the corresponding fingers of a pair of gloves at the first attempt. No matter how carefully and cautiously you approach the task in hand, you will inevitably end up with at least one digit-less glove finger, and at least one glove finger over-supplied with the little blighters. What's worse is that the second attempt usually ends up in the same farrago.

Tears often ensue. (And your child can get pretty upset too.)

REASON

All children respond to reason. They respond by ignoring what you're saying and carrying on doing what they're doing.

DISCIPLINE

Incentivise your child by rewarding them with sweets whenever they do something good. Punish them when they are naughty by making them eat vegetables.

STRESS AT MEALTIMES
Mealtimes with small children can easily become a battlefield. Avoid this by encouraging relaxation. Do this by drinking a large gin and tonic ten minutes before the meal and a larger one during it.

A FACT OF LIFE
Everyone else's buggy always looks cleaner than yours.

WHAT FIDEL CASTRO, HO CHI MINH AND YOUR BABY HAVE IN COMMON

It's all to do with strategy and tactics. Fidel overthrew the ruling regime in Cuba after landing on the island with little more than a handful of raw revolutionaries. Uncle Ho masterminded the ultimately triumphant resistance of a third world country of rice farmers against the most powerful war machine in the history of the world. Both achieved their aims by the judicious and audacious use of guerilla tactics.

They staged hit and run raids.

They ignored all conventional rules of conflict. They turned their enemies strengths against them. They constantly redefined the arena of conflict so as to catch the opposition unawares. They knew no fear. And they seemed to have no regard for their own personal safety.

These are all strategies and tactics that you, as a parent, will soon become familiar with as you get bogged down in the endless campaign that is rearing your child. You see, what you are engaged in is not the seemingly straightforward endeavour of 'parenting', but instead a fundamental clash between two mutually exclusive ideologies just as intense as the conflict waged between capitalism and communism.

And if you think the relatively 'hot war' of parenting a baby is draining, just wait until the 'Cold War' of parenting a teenager kicks off.

BRUSHING TEETH

Encourage your child to use a toothbrush by starting them off with chocolate spread on it. When the time is right, substitute with toothpaste.

'HE'S ONLY FIFTEEN MONTHS AND HE'S ALREADY WALKING/TALKING/HELPING HIS FATHER WITH HIS TAX RETURN!'

There will always be one parent in your circle of friends whose child is, developmentally speaking, way ahead of yours. This will inevitably make you feel defensive and inadequate and that there's something wrong with your child. Worry not. These seemingly 'advanced' children are in fact highly trained midgets planted with bogus parents by a shadowy and sinister capitalist cabal headed by

Mothercare and The Early Learning Centre. Their aim is to 'persuade' you that for your child to 'catch up', you must, as a really caring parent empty your purse/wallet/ savings account and blindly buy anything that carries the words 'helps development' on the box.

BONDING

Before you have your child, it is only natural for you to wonder what the mysterious mechanism that will bond you and your child together will be. After you have your child, you'll soon realise that it's not some magical, intangible 'emotional glue' that effects the bonding but a bonding agent that's much more real. It's called snot. And it gets on your clothes, in your hair and all over your house. It's snot so hard to shift that it makes superglue look like the haphazard product of a bunch of clueless amateurs.

YET ANOTHER ONE OF THOSE IRRITATING LAWS

The more grumpy your child becomes on the way to the playground, the longer will the queue be to get on the swings.

THE 50% RULE OF FRESH FRUIT AND VEG

At least 50 per cent of the fresh fruit and veg you buy, whenever the urge overcomes you to try and get your child to eat something healthy, will rot before you get round to using it.

RUNNING AWAY

If your child constantly runs away each time you put them down, don't worry. This is a common behavioural pattern that many experts see as indicating that the child has confidence that you will be there when they get back. However, if your child runs away, boards a bus, train or aeroplane, gets out in another city, or indeed country, changes their name and sets up a mail order company selling hair-care products, you may have a problem.

FORGET THE WHEEL, FIRE, OR THE TV REMOTE CONTROL

The greatest invention of all time?
Wet wipes. No contest.

THE NON-COLLAPSING COLLAPSIBLE PUSHCHAIR ANOMALY

Be forewarned that your collapsible pushchair will always decide not to collapse whenever, whilst struggling with two full carrier bags of shopping and one small child hell-bent on escape, you try to get on a crowded bus.

ONE OF THE BITTERSWEET IRONIES OF LIFE WITH SMALL CHILDREN

For every parent there is a blissful, peace -filled oasis of tranquillity after your child has finally gone to bed, and before you retire for the night. This is true quality time for you and your partner.

Unfortunately, you will always be too knackered to do little more than veg out in front of whatever mindless rubbish spews forth from the TV, too shattered to even change the channel.

HOW TO COMBINE A SUCCESSFUL CAREER WITH BEING A SUCCESSFUL PARENT

Sounds good in principle, doesn't it?

RAISINS TO BE CHEERFUL

In strict economic terms they make very little sense. But, frankly, as a parent, economic sense will lie way in the distant past.

Hence you will happily pay over the odds for all manner of things that you would once never have even considered buying. Like convenience foods. After all, surely a few additives and preservatives and day-glo food colourings can't be that bad for them? And at least they eat the stuff.

Then you discover that some genius has packaged raisins in tiny little boxes that are so cute they fool small people into thinking that they're eating sweets. And your mind races round the dog track that goes 'raisins are grapes and grapes are fruit and fruit is healthy!' Hurrah!

Now all we need is someone to package broccoli, carrots and spinach in the same way and we'll all be laughing.

IT'S GOOD TO TALK

For the sake of good mental health, hard though it is, it is vital that you have at least one conversation per day that doesn't revolve around your child. If necessary, arrange visits by Jehovah's Witnesses or those people who come round wanting to know whether you want to change your gas supply.

THE POPULATION EXPLOSION. WHY THE PLANET IS IN DANGER AND STING SHOULD DO A CONCERT

It is projected that if the world's population of soft toys keeps growing at the current rate then at some point within the next twenty years the entire land surface of the earth will be covered in a debilitating layer of cuddliness, three teddy bears deep.

WHEN SIBLES QUIBBLE. LESS A CASE OF PARENTING, MORE A DESPERATE ATTEMPT AT POLICING AND CONTAINMENT

It is standard practice among the more enlightened police forces around the globe when confronted with, and out-numbered by, a mass of rioters, to try and confine the rowdies and hence the damage to a limited area. In many ways siblings, in full-on quibbling mode, are much like rioters. They are fast, manouevrable, intent on damage (both to persons and property), pay no heed to rules, and are not amenable to reason.

As I have yet to come across a branch of Mothercare which stocks rubber bullets or water cannons this presents you with a particular problem. And I wish I could tell you what the solution is. Unfortunately my attempts at policing rapidly escalated from the parental equivalent of Dixon Of Dock Green giving a ne'er do well a hard stare and going ''Ello, 'ello. 'ello, what's going on 'ere then?' to the threatened summoning of a UN sponsored international peace keeping force. (In this case Uncle Keith, as in, 'if you don't start behaving I'll send for Uncle Keith.')

It was a threat that earned but a temporary respite from the mayhem).

So my only advice is to follow the lead of the world's police forces and try and contain the damage. And if all else fails, while they're distracted by their activities, move house.

REGRESSION

At some point in the whole fraught affair you will encounter a period of regression. This involves wanting to be looked after and treated like a helpless baby. You really should resist this. After all, you are the adult.

HOW DID THAT GET THERE?

It is a law of nature that every small child should have a certain quantity of grains of sand adhering to their scalp at all times, no matter how many months ago they last visited a beach or a sandpit.

BIRTHDAY PRESENTS AND CHRISTMAS PRESENTS.
A UNIVERSAL TRUTH

The box and the wrapping will always be more interesting than whatever's inside it.

NO CONTEST

A cupboard full of toys vs a
saucepan and a lid.

FAST FOOD

When visiting friends for a meal
with your offspring you will, to your
horror, discover that you have
developed the ability to eat
everything on your plate in the time
it takes the other, child-free adults,
to take one mouthful and initiate a
conversation about the latest movie
that you know you won't catch
until it's out on video.

HOW TO SPEND A WHOLE DAY WITHOUT YELLING AT YOUR KIDS

Sneak out early before they get up. Return home after they've gone to bed.

STAIRGATES

Stairgates are designed to prevent small children going up and down stairs. They work for about two weeks. After that your child will have figured out how to open them. They are, however, completely baffling to visiting adult friends and relatives. Before any such people arrive it's advisable to remove the stairgate from the stairs, or you'll spend the rest of the visit waiting for the inevitable crashing sound.

BATTERIES

The only thing that runs down quicker than the batteries in most electronic toys is your patience with the cacophony of horrendous squeaks, shrieks and sound effects that they produce.

ON THE FUNDAMENTAL DECEPTIVE NATURE OF 'THE WHEELS ON THE BUS'

The cheery conviviality of the song 'The Wheels On The Bus' gives a completely false impression of the degree of warmth with which you will be greeted with by conductors and passengers alike should you attempt to board a crowded bus with your buggy during the rush hour.

PORRIDGE

Never let uneaten porridge dry in a bowl. If you do, you will need a pneumatic drill to shift it.

OH DEAR COLOGNE
No amount of perfume or aftershave, no matter how industrial its strength, can mask the fragrance of milk on your clothes slowly heading cheesewards.

CALPOL
Thank you, God.

NON-STOP WHINING
No-one likes it. And no-one really cares how hard you find it coping with your own particular child.

HIDING
Honestly, I know how you feel. But eventually you have to come out and get on with the parenting.

130

DIFFERENT STATES OF BEING

Scientists have long known that different things have different, naturally occurring, states of being. Hence water is a liquid, oxygen is gas and iron is a solid. A small child's naturally occurring state of being is something far more permanent than any of these forms of being.

It's grubbiness.

BEFORE AND AFTER PARENTHOOD. A SMUGNESS CHECK

Remember how you had made the decision to opt for a natural childbirth without an epidural until the full horror of the actual experience had you flinging your principles away from you faster than an ambitious politician sniffing the possibility of power? That's exactly how your attitude to McDonald's Happy Meals will change after you have a small child.

SIX REASONS WHY A BABY MIGHT BE CRYING

1. Hunger
2. Anxiety
3. Pain
4. Frustration
5. Overtiredness
6. Because they know it really winds you up.

HEARING PROBLEMS

The most common hearing problem
with small children is Highly
Selective Parental Deafness (HSPD).
In this, the small child is unable to
hear any instructions or
admonitions given by the parent
but has no difficulty hearing the
approaching chimes of an ice-cream
van anything up to half a time zone
away.

IMAGINARY FRIENDS

Many small children have imaginary friends. Bizarrely, as the parent of a small child, you will discover that you see some of your friends so rarely (especially those without children themselves) that you too have to resort to imagining them.

JIGSAWS

After just one solitary outing from its box, even the most simple of jigsaws will have one piece missing. Pre-empt this calamity by, before you allow your child to play with it for the first time, removing a piece and keeping it somewhere safe.

EVEN CARAVAGGIO HAD TO START SOMEWHERE

Be warned that the first time your child draws a picture of you it won't be very accurate. It'll probably resemble nothing more than a blob with squiggles and maybe a couple of dots. Try not to be too overcritical.

CHILD PSYCHOLOGY

All small children are expert psychologists. They know how your mind works and how to manipulate it. They are particularly good at discovering and exploiting weak spots in your resolve. And when it comes to controlling two seemingly all powerful parents, they are miniature Machiavellis in the deployment of the tactics and strategies of the 'divide and rule' approach.

WHAT GOES AROUND, COMES AROUND

It is a fundamental truth that any cough, sniffle or sneeze that is coughed, sniffled or sneezed by any small child within a rather surprisingly large geographic area will eventually establish a residency within your small child. There is no way of avoiding this. So there is no point in worrying about it. But you will worry, anyway. It's one of the perks of being a parent.

As a footnote to this observation, I would add that parents commonly make the mistake of thinking that if they wrap up a small child in more layers of warm clothing than you would find packed for the entire complement of a ten-man, three-month expedition to Antarctica, that they can prevent infection. This, unfortunately, is not how things work.

However, when said children are so attired, it takes but a little imagination, some forward planning and a chalk circle drawn in the ground to organise a mini sumo wrestling tournament.

WHY CHILDREN SIT TOO CLOSE TO THE TELEVISION

It's a CinemaScope thing.

WHY SMALL CHILDREN CAN BE AS IRRITATING AS CERTAIN CELEBRITIES

Because they seek attention all the time. And they don't care how annoyingly they act in order to get it.

WHAT IS DISCIPLINE?

Discipline is learning to resist the urge to smack your child when they have done something very naughty or dangerous.

THE BALANCED DIET PROBLEM

Human beings need six different types of nourishment to survive: protein, carbohydrates, fats, vitamins, minerals and water. As far as small children are concerned, their list is somewhat different: crisps, chocolate, ice-cream, chips, fizzy drinks and small bits of plastic or gunk foraged from the floor.

It is in the mismatch between these varying approaches to nutrition that problems can arise.

NO MATTER HOW BLUE THE SKY

The minute you finish blowing up and filling up the paddling pool, the sun will go in.

LOST CAUSES

It is easier to find a popular traffic warden than a lost sock in a ball pond.

IN A CLASSROOM FULL OF CORDELIAS WILL IT BE THE MARY'S WHO GET LAUGHED AT?

As you start attending activity groups with your child you will realise that the coming generation have a most 'diverse' selection of names. Literary, historical and just plain odd choices litter the place like herring in a hurricane. Call your child John, Janet, Mary or Michael and you run the risk of saddling your beloved with not so much a name, as a lifelong reminder of just what an unimaginative individual you truly are.

In order to avoid this, I have

gathered together a selection of names that you can feel free to substitute for your child's existing name safe in the knowledge that they will out-odd anything that Osric and Persephone's mummy and daddy could come up with over the Chardonnay.

BOYS NAMES
Coelacanth
Fetish
Psimon
Wetherby
Pharyngeal

GIRLS NAMES
Jojoba
Couscous
Orangina
Arugula
Segue

Alternatively, christen your child 'Gap' and you will find that a constantly changing selection of personalised clothing will be yours for a very reasonable price, especially if you wait to get things in the seemingly never-ending sales.

'SHARE'
A word that has the same effect on small children that garlic does on vampires.

IT ALL DEPENDS ON YOUR POINT OF VIEW

To you it's a small sandpit for the garden. To the neighbourhood cats it's a most stylish and commodious litter tray.

BOLTERS AND LIMPETS

Small children often fall into these two distinct categories. Limpets are characteristically found clamped to your leg all the time you are trying to do even the simplest of tasks. They typically engender intermittent feelings of great frustration and annoyance in their parents.

Bolters are characteristically found only after much frantic searching. Hence the predominant states of mind of the parent of a bolter are stress and worry.

Whichever category your child falls into, you will wish you had one of the other sort. However, if your child displays behaviour that puts them into the rare, but not unheard of, bolter-limpet category, then my heart goes out to you.

BOLTER-WEAR

If your child is a bolter then I'm afraid that sartorial elegance and understated elan are not really sensible options when it comes to dressing them for outdoor excursions. Instead go for bright, garish and ideally fluorescent colours. And, if possible, secrete a satellite tracking navigation system about their person.

'I'LL BE SITTING HERE'

No matter where you position yourself in a playground your child will decide to play in the one spot you can't see.

THE GRASS IS ALWAYS GREENER

For any small child the most interesting toy is always the one someone else is playing with.

AND YOU THOUGHT IAN PAISLEY WAS LOUD

There is no correlation between the size of a child and the volume that it can produce.

THE ELASTIC NATURE OF TIME

You will be able to cram more in the two hours that your baby naps than you used to in a whole day when you were child-free. Indeed you know that saying 'Rome wasn't built in a day'? Well I reckon it could easily have been if they'd only had twelve parents on the job, each working the two-hour shift when their kids were asleep.

158

FLYING PIGS AND THE LIKE

For two or more small children, 'playing nicely' for a period longer than 30 or 40 seconds is about as likely as the arrival of Godot round at Samuel Beckett's house.

WHY YOU SOMETIMES HEAR SONIC BOOMS IN PLAYGROUNDS

Even the US men's sprint relay team have got nothing on the average parent spotting their toddler heading unchecked towards an occupied and fast moving swing.

LIGHTS! CAMERA! INACTION!

Once you have a baby you will not see a movie again at the cinema for at least two years. But worry not, because below you will find a summary of the outcome of all the movies you will miss, along with some critical analyses that will enable you to join in the conversations of friends who have seen the movies:

1. If it's a Hollywood romantic comedy then, despite a series of hilarious obstacles and misunderstandings, the boy will eventually get the girl.

2. If it's a Hollywood thriller then a lot of people will get shot, things will get spectacularly blown up, but the hero will win through and eventually get the girl.

3. If it's a Hollywood Second World War movie there will be even more explosions, the generalised feeling that war is bad and a failure to mention the fact that the Americans didn't actually fight the war on their own. The hero will win through having lost close buddies in the process. And will eventually get the girl.

4. If it's a French movie, there will be lots of quirky observations on

life. A plot that pretends to be sophisticated. Plenty of cigarette smoking. And eventually the girl will get the girl.

5. If it's a British movie then, despite the rave quotes on the poster it will be kind of disappointing.

6. If it's a special effects movie then the special effects will be mind blowing, but the plot will be mind-numbing.

7. If it's a Tom Hanks movie then it will be entertaining but hardly earth-shattering and you won't understand why he's been nominated for an Oscar.

8. If it's the much-hyped first movie of the new cinema wonder kid it will be pretty good, have great performances by actors who aren't big stars, but on reflection turn out to be pretty thin in many areas beneath its dazzling surface, and generally not as good as it was built up to be.
9. If it's the eagerly awaited second movie of the new cinema wonder kid then it won't be as good as his first.
10. If it's by Nick Park it'll be a work of considerable genius.

HOW SUBTLE DIFFERENCES CAN MEAN A LOT

To you or I 'dressing up' may seem almost identical an activity to 'getting dressed' but to a small child they are vastly different. Hence the former will be happily indulged in for hours on end, while the latter will be resisted with a resolve that even Robert The Bruce would admire. Especially if you're in a hurry to go somewhere.

A THING TO DO AT 5AM

Curse yourself for not getting satellite or cable or anything else with a 24-hour cartoon network.

SEEING RED

No matter how hard you resist it on account of your lifelong aversion to and struggle against gender stereotyping, there will come a point in your life as a parent when you have to admit defeat in the face of a universal truth.

Girls like pink.

WHY BABIES AND SMALL CHILDREN BOND WITH GRANDPARENTS

Because that way they can outmanoeuvre you in a classic pincer movement.

THE BEST SONGS FOR CHILDREN

This is what children like in a song:

1. A simple tune.
2. A small number of words.
3. Lines or phrases that are repeated.
4. Sounds or animal noises interjected at certain points.
5. Hand movements or actions that illustrate the song.

Heavy metal, in other words.

CRASH!
Babies love knocking down and demolishing things like piles of bricks, or books on a shelf, or the idea that you and your partner were going to share childcare duties evenly.

UPWARDLY MOBILE

This refers to the way you will have to constantly move your mobile phone to higher and higher resting places to avoid it being used as a bangy thing by small, grasping hands.

INDELIBLE

The dyes and colourings used in the manufacture of ice lollies produce stains that even a week-long soak in sulphuric acid do nothing to shift.

OVERTIRED

A ludicrous turn of events that finally proves that we live in an Alice In Wonderland world where black can be white, up can be down and Tony Blair can win a landslide victory with less votes than Neil Kinnock got when he lost.

Basically your child gets so tired that they can't go to sleep. Figure that one out.

100-1 AGAINST
The chances of you finishing any book you start reading.

WASTE NOT, WAIST A LOT

The urge to taste your children's food as you prepare it, or finish off what they leave is universal and irresistible. After all it's so much more appealing than the grown-up food you're going to eat later. That's why dieting and parenting go to together like Malibu and mustard.

TRANSITIONAL COMFORT OBJECTS

These are things that provide comfort and reassurance in times of stress and uncertainty. For instance, babies will often cling to an old cot blanket or a particular cuddly toy. Parents, on the other hand, cling to a cigarette, a large brandy, or the idea that at some point things are going to settle down and get easier to cope with.

THE ARCHED BACK OR STIFF-AS-A-BOARD BODY

The ultimate non co-operation tactic deployed by seasoned campaigners when they don't want to get in the high chair, car seat or get dressed or undressed.

LANGUAGE DEVELOPMENT

Children learn words by hearing the emphasis placed on them. So when you say to them 'elephant' they hear 'efant', hence that's what they say. But surprisingly, when you say to them 'Oh my God, you've ruined my life, I used to be a successful, happy, adult going places in my job, but now I'm a physical and emotional wreck with my career in ruins, porridge all over my clothes and I haven't had sex since I can't remember when', they hear very little.

ON BABIES AND BATHS
It is generally frowned upon to test the temperature of your baby's bath using your baby.

THE ONE UNFAILING MIGRATORY PATTERN EVEN DAVID ATTENBOROUGH SEEMS TO HAVE MISSED

There are the huge swarms of wildebeest in their annual trek across the Serengeti. There is the amazing endeavour of salmon leaping up fast-running streams to return to their birthplace to mate.

And then there's the mysterious appearance of hordes of slightly uncomfortable-looking fathers around the sandpits and swings of playgrounds every Saturday and Sunday.

CLEANLINESS

If the pile of discarded food around your baby's high chair has reached their feet, it's probably time to clean up.

HOW CAN YOU MAKE EATING OUT WITH SMALL CHILDREN LESS STRESSFUL?

Move to Italy.

IN THE BALANCE

Parenting has often been described as a balancing act. There's the balance between discipline and indulgence. There's the balance between allowing your child to experience the world independently and making sure they don't try anything too dangerous. And there is the extremely tricky balance to maintain between broccoli and Mars bars. (N.B. broccoli and Mars bars are used in this context to symbolise the whole vegetable vs sweets conundrum).

There is, however, a more literal balancing act that you as a parent will have to master. It's the one that you'll find yourself involved in when your beloved little cherub is having 'difficulty' sleeping at three in the morning and you stupidly think to yourself 'I know, let's get them in to bed with us'.

Now whether you have a double bed, a queen-size bed, a king-size bed or a god-emperor/master-of-the universe-size bed, the result will be the same. You'll end up perched precariously on a sliver of mattress narrower than a sideways-on After Eight mint.

NON-SPILL CUPS
Don't believe the hype.

WHAT THE INSTRUCTIONS FOR THE CAR SEAT WON'T TELL YOU
That they're impossible to fit
without pouring with sweat.

THE DEVELOPMENT OF HAND TO EYE CO-ORDINATION.

All babies have the ability, from a very early age, to co-ordinate their hand into your eye.

ICE CREAM? WHY SCREAM?

For the sake of your sanity just accept the fact that they're never going to eat an ice cream fast enough so that it doesn't drip over everything, or remember not to tip it sideways so that ice cream falls out of the cone.

BECAUSE IT'S THERE

A parent with clean clothing is an irresistible challenge to any small child with a grubby hand or a snotty nose.

'ARE WE THERE YET?'

On long car journeys babies and small children know that it will annoy you most if they stay awake and whinge for the entire duration of the trip, but fall asleep the second that you get to where you're going.

'MY MOTHER THINKS I'M DOING
IT ALL WRONG, SHOULD I
LISTEN TO HER?'
No.

AND FINALLY, FIVE WORDS OR PHRASES YOU MAY FIND USEFUL

1. No!
2. Gently!
3. Mind Your Fingers!
4. *********! (Insert name of child).
5. Pass the wine.

An extract from Rohan Candappa's bestselling
AUTOBIOGRAPHY OF A ONE YEAR OLD

'Adrian Mole and Harry Potter can forget it' *The Times*
'Hilarious' *Helen Fielding*

CHAPTER 2

WHO WILL RID ME OF THIS TROUBLESOME DARK?

Dark. I'm not entirely sure that I've got a handle on it.

Dark mainly turns up when you're tired. It kind of lurks about, in the corners of places, biding its time. Then the very second your eyelids droop, dark's in like a shot. If you don't want dark to take over you have to act fast. Force those eyelids open. Because the second dark sees you opening your eyes it tends to back off.

But even though it's backed off, it hasn't gone far. It tends to sneak away and hides. Dark loves being under things. The other day I found loads of the stuff under the cot. That night when I went to bed, it was still there. I've also noticed that dark hides behind curtains. So when, of an evening, Hairy or Smooth pulls the curtains together dark floods out and starts to fill the room. Then, in the morning, when they open the curtains, dark rushes back to hide in the folds.

Dark hates certain switches. If you can get your hands on any of these switches you've pretty much got dark on the run. Unfortunately these switches, as well as being at a stupid height, appear to be the parents' own personal playthings. If they ever spot you near one of these switches, you're soon whisked away.

Now we come to the thorny issue of whether or not I'm afraid the dark. It may appear to the less astute observer, on account of my regular wailing when dark turns up, that I am, indeed, afraid of the dark. For the record, I must state that I am unequivocally not afraid of the dark. I wail because of the limitations the dark puts upon me. It's quite hard to see things in the dark. And because it's quite hard to see things, it's quite hard to do things. And that's what upsets me. It's not the possibility of what might happen to me in the dark, but the impossibility of the things I can't do on account of the fact that I can't see what the hell's going on.

It's all about lost opportunities. Don't tell me you haven't ever cried over a lost opportunity. Life is short, and I've no time to waste. There are sandpits to conquer, shelves to pull down, books to shred and rusks to chew up and drop all over the house. So I've no time for this dark malarkey. I'm a very busy baby.

PTO to order a copy now!

All Ebury titles are available in good bookshops or via mail order

TO ORDER (please tick)

The Little Book of Stress	£2.50	❐
The Little Book of Wrong Shui	£2.50	❐
Stress for Success	£2.50	❐
The Little Book of The Kama Sutra	£2.50	❐
Autobiography of a One Year Old	£5.99	❐
Growing Old Disgracefully (published 1/8/02)	£4.99	❐

PAYMENT MAY BE MADE USING ACCESS, VISA, MASTERCARD, DINERS CLUB, SWITCH AND AMEX OR CHEQUE, EUROCHEQUE AND POSTAL ORDER (STERLING ONLY)

CARD NUMBER:

EXPIRY DATE:........................   SWITCH ISSUE NO:......................

SIGNATURE:..

PLASE ALLOW £2.50 FOR POST AND PACKAGING FOR THE FIRST BOOK AND £1.00 THEREAFTER

ORDER TOTAL: £   (INC P&P)

ALL ORDERS TO:

EBURY PRESS, BOOKS BY POST, TBS LIMITED, COLCHESTER ROAD, FRATING GREEN, COLCHESTER, ESSEX CO7 7DW, UK

TELEHONE: 01206 256 000
FAX: 01206 255 914

NAME:

ADDRESS:

Please allow 28 days for delivery.

❐ Please tick box if you do not wish to receive any additional information

Prices and availability subject to change without notice.